ERION P

Bold

AND BEAUTIFUL

6 THINGS EVERY FEMALE SHOULD KNOW

DEDICATION

I dedicate this book to every female that feels invisible

at times. To every female that has ever felt

worthless, broken, and forsaken,

I dedicate this book to you. Know that you are not alone in

this battle called life. Before the foundation of world,

God declared you,

Bold
AND BEAUTIFUL.

PATRICIA BIRD

You are the foundation of our family. I love you grandmother and you will forever be in my heart.

you are my foundation.

ANGELA BIRD

There's no greater mom in the world. Everything I am today is because o the love you have shown me since the beginning of time. One thing I kno for sure is that you are the one that will have my back until the end of time I love you mommy. When I tell you, "I Love You," I don't say it out of hab or to make conversation. I say it to remind you that YOU are the Best Thin that ever happened to me.

you are my everything.

DEIDRE BAZILE

You may be surprised that you're on this list, but you are truly a special au in my life. Thank you for ALWAYS supporting me no matter what. You & your family constantly travel 903 miles round trip to make sure you are he for EVERY event I have. I will never be able to pay you back for all you have done for me, but I must say THANK YOU.
Love you Deedy from Lil Rat!

you are my support.

JOCELYN CARRAL

You are my personal hustler for my business. LOL. You always speak with business owners, influential people in the city to help me as your niece. I may not always say it but I really appreciate that. Love you Aunt!

you are my hustler.

BRENDA DEGGINS

You are a second mother to me. When I was a little girl you bought me nything I wanted and even bought things I never asked for. I never have to question your love for me because your love ALWAYS comes with action. Thank you for being the world's best God-Mom. I know this is a book for adies, but I must also acknowledge the world's best God-Father. I love you both and I hope I am making you proud.

you are my encourager.

> "INDIVIDUALLY, WE ARE ONE DROP, BUT
>
> TOGETHER WE ARE AN OCEAN."
>
> - *Ryunosuke Satoro*

None of this would be possible without my family...

Erion Davison, Angela Bird, Erek Davison, Earea Davison, Erica Scott

"PEOPLE COME AND PEOPLE
GO IN OUR LIVES BUT A
BEAUTY OF LIFE IS THAT OUR
FAMILY IS ALWAYS THERE."

— Erion P. Davison

table of CONTENTS

A NOTE FROM THE AUTHOR

ERION P. DAVISON

In this book, we will discuss six important things I believe every female **needs** to know. Let me begin by saying I don't believe I, or even this book has all the answers concerning the life of a female. I do believe that these top six areas that I mention in the book are some of the most crucial facts that every female needs to accept about her life. This isn't a book where you find me as a hero or I do anything *so* amazing or out of the ordinary, but this is a book that is completely honest about my experiences as a female so far. As you began to read this book, I challenge you to read every word, every line, and every chapter in a personal way. See yourself on these pages. May my transparency and truthfulness help every girl, teenager, young lady, and grown woman that reads these pages. Whether you're a daughter, a mom, an aunt, a grandmother, or a sister there's something in this book that has the ability to change your life.

Chapter 1 here we come...

NOT A MISTAKE.

I released my very first book at 16 years old and the results have blown my mind. I am still surprised at the great accomplishments and recognition my first book has afforded me thus far. I don't want anyone to believe that because I am a young author and I have accomplished some pretty cool things that I believe that I have arrived in life. I still have a long way to go. The truth is whether you're blessed or broke, you will still have some things to overcome. Whether you're rich or poor you will have some things to overcome. Even in the season of great blessings, I still have a war to fight with myself at times. I remember when the books sales were doing great. I remember last year on my weekly book tour when hundreds would buy my book and I would be able to receive thousands of dollars within 120 minutes on a Sunday. Sounds great, right? Well money, riches, or success will never be the answer to accepting the fact that **you have a purpose**.

"As well as my book did and is still doing, I remember *questioning myself as a mistake*."

I remember applying for my first published book to be accepted into a well-known international bookstore and I was indeed excited. I will never forget the day I received those results. My mom opened the letter and showed me that our request was

DENIED.

I sat there with an expression on my face as if everything was alright, but to be completely honest on the inside I began to once again question my purpose.

According to a particular dictionary the word "MISTAKE" means to be wrong. The original word for mistake is *Mistaca*, which is defined as "to take in error." Ladies, when you believe you are a mistake you automatically (intentionally or unintentionally) inform God that He made an error when He created you. In Jeremiah 29:11, it states, *"For I know the plans I have for you,"* declares the LORD, *"plans to prosper you and not to harm you, plans to give you hope and a future."*

Do you feel that you are a mistake or that something about you is wrong?

Ladies, if this is you, I want you to say these 5 words with confidence and boldness. "I AM NOT A MISTAKE!" You must believe that God has you on this Earth for a reason no matter how many times you failed at something. No matter how many times you did more negative than positive, you must accept the fact that you are not a mistake! Some of you may say "my dreams and goals haven't come to reality, so there must be something wrong with me." Because of the rejection I faced from the international book company I believed that my book "Keep Running" was a mistake, and **even me** because I wrote it. Do you see what happened? I was excited when everyone loved my book, but the moment I received a "NO" I felt rejected. Ladies, never let Satan play with your mind when you receive a no, and you were expecting a yes. **Don't ever forget that denial from people doesn't cancel the plan that God has for your life.** Rejection from people is an opportunity for God to be God in your life. Don't sweat the denials, the rejections, or even the dismissals. God is going to use ALL of that for your good.

Ladies, you have a purpose even when you receive tough news. I allowed a letter of denial to change my entire attitude. Don't give bad situations permission to interrupt the goodness God is doing in your life. Don't get me wrong. I know I came from God and I was made in His image. I know that God spoke to me about writing the book, but for a moment I began to doubt EVERYTHING. Satan will try to use bad moments to put you in an even worse position doubting God. *Moments are for a season, but misery tries to stay for a lifetime.* Don't let the few bad moments keep you in misery forever. Get out of that place and do it QUICK. If you entertain the negativity, you will stay in a low place for too long. I had to remind myself that I still had a purpose even after the denial letter. Rejection from others isn't a sign that you should quit. It is only redirection from God that there is something greater in store for your life. So never take a "no" personal, it's part of a bigger plan for you to receive your permanent "yes!" If God will answer your prayer that's not connected to His purpose for your life, it would be a complete waste of time. What you ask for would only be temporary because it is not in alignment with His bigger plan for your life. The good news is that God would never give you something that you ask for that doesn't connect to His purpose for your life. God is more concerned about your future than your feelings. Remember this: **God KNOWS what He is doing.** He has it all planned out. So the rejection from man will never catch him by surprise. Everything will be okay. I challenge you to seek God and make sure your plan lines up with His purpose for your life. Ladies, some of the most miserable women are living their lives doing something they were never created to do, and now they are frustrated with their current situations. If this is you, I challenge you, reroute, turn around and get on the path that God has layed out for you. That denial letter was my very first "no." I was still determined to make an impact in the lives of people. The denial indeed did hurt, but I refuse to let it stop me. Know that God has a distinct and divine purpose for your life.

The purpose that God has for your life will be worth all the rejection you will receive during the process. I told you my story because you need to know that even after all of the rejection, your life still matters. I must also say that denial letter has given me even more focus to make sure that one day my book will be in the same store that it was rejected by. I realized that I only have to work harder to ensure that every dream that I have becomes a reality.

Are you the female that feels like you're not supposed to be here because of your mom and dad's mistakes?

You may feel as though you are a mistake because they didn't plan for you to be here, it just happened. Maybe you're the lady that was rejected by your father and now you're a grown woman still dealing with the hurt of who didn't love you. Maybe you're the young lady who seeks attention from people and will do whatever it takes to get someone to notice you. Well I have news for you. Even though your parents may not have planned for you to be here, God allowed it. Maybe you're dating, maybe you're married, maybe you're divorced, or maybe you're a widow and because of the rejection from someone that you loved, you now believe your life doesn't matter. Maybe you've been taken advantage of by your boyfriend, your fiancé, your spouse or just believe that your life isn't important because of what they did. Maybe you're the lady that constantly lives her life in a cycle. You are constantly doing the same things over and over again. Maybe you're a teenage girl that feels invisible at home because your parents may not acknowledge you. Maybe they work so much that they barely see you. Many females that live their life in circles believe they are not enough because someone they loved left them. You must stop the cycle and understand that your parents may not have planned for you, but God has always had a plan for you. Nothing ever catches God by surprise. The Bible says in Isaiah 45:18 "I made you and will take care of you". It doesn't matter what others think about your existence **you have a reason to be on this Earth.** If you didn't, you would've never been born in the Earth. Accept this ladies: you had a purpose before people had an opinion.

YOU ARE NOT A MISTAKE.

Let's Pray:

Father God, thank you for helping me identify what you created me to be. God thank you for thinking of me even before my mom or dad knew me. I know that I am not a mistake because I wouldn't be born if I was. God give me the strength that I need to be able to move forward when someone rejects me and I feel like nothing. God help me embrace the process to reach my full potential. Help me deal with the mental battle of accepting that I have a God-given purpose from you. Lord, let my desire to fulfill your purpose for my life be greater than my own selfish goals. God give me a clear understanding what the difference is between careers and calling. Whatever your purpose is for my life, let me be obedient to your purpose no matter what.

Amen.

"LADIES' LIFELINES"

SCRIPTURES TO REMEMBER

"I praise you, for I am fearfully and wonderfully made. Wonderful are your works; my soul knows it very well."

Psalm 139:14

"So God created man in his own image, in the image of God he created him; male and female he created them."

Genesis 1:27

JOURNAL

YOU ARE NOT A MISTAKE.

What mistakes have you made in your life? Have you fully recovered from them? If so, what did you do? If not, what's holding you back?

_____

_____

_____

_____

_____

_____

_____

_____

_____

_____

_____

_____

_____

_____

_____

_____

_____

_____

_____

FACT NUMBER ONE

FACT NUMBER ONE

_____

_____

_____

_____

_____

_____

_____

_____

_____

_____

_____

_____

_____

_____

_____

_____

_____

_____

_____

_____

_____

_____

_____

FACT NUMBER ONE

_____

_____

_____

_____

_____

_____

_____

_____

_____

_____

_____

_____

_____

_____

_____

_____

_____

_____

_____

_____

_____

_____

_____

_____

_____

_____

_____

_____

_____

_____

_____

_____

_____

_____

_____

_____

_____

_____

_____

_____

_____

_____

_____

_____

_____

_____

FACT NUMBER ONE

FACT NUMBER ONE

you ARE...

FORGIVEN.

Are you the female that feels like you're not forgiven, because of the mistakes you have made? Are you the female after a bad decision you no longer know where to turn or where to go? Are you the grown lady that feels like God can't forgive you anymore because you made the same wrong decisions even as a little girl? Maybe you feel like you have done wrong for so long that rights no longer exist inside of you. Maybe you are girl that attempts to do right, but wrong feel so much easier. Maybe you're at a point in your life that wrong-living is so easy that you no longer look for guidance from others to begin to do the right thing.

Well, God sent me to tell you some pretty cool and amazing news and that is…*you are forgiven.* Maybe you ask, how do you know? Trust me I know. I believe that in order for me to really be able to help ladies of all ages in this book I have to be completely honest and transparent. In my previous book, I discussed dating a boy in middle school and the relationship that had a drastic impact on my life. In that particular chapter, I talked about dating someone that didn't have my best interest at heart. He was someone that pulled me away from my purpose, and even someone that tried to rape and molest me. That's horrible, right? I totally agree it is. Even though his rape attempt was unsuccessful because someone came to my rescue right on time (and I thank God everyday for protecting me in that particular situation) I also had to forgive myself for what I did. There were times when my ex-boyfriend would ask me to Facetime him so he can see me naked. Immediately when he asked I said NO! He would continually ask and I would repeatedly say NO! Until one day I got tired of the same question, so I gave in. I couldn't believe what I said yes to do. I felt horrible, I felt empty, I felt stupid, I felt dumb, I felt exposed, and I felt completely embarrassed. At this time in my life, God and I certainly didn't have a relationship, but I still knew this wasn't right. I felt like I disappointed everyone that loved me and everyone I loved as well. I felt like I really disappointed my mother. Let me pause everything and say: Parents your children will do things that is completely opposite of what you have instilled in them growing up. I want to stop and encourage every parent that feels like "where did I go wrong?" The truth is, you didn't go wrong. Your child did. I know this is one of the most disappointing things that I ever had to share with my mom (and trust me, she was disappointed). Girls, be careful of the decisions you make because it is a reflection of the people you call "mommy" and "daddy." Even though my mom never gave me the consent to make such a horrible decision, indirectly, it was a reflection of her. Through it all, she still loves me. Now don't get me wrong, she wanted to kill me. But she still loves me. Parents, I believe, the worst thing you can do to your daughter after she reveals an ugly truth, is to receive it in a manner that causes her to shut down and never be transparent with you again. I am not saying you don't have the right to be upset, but there is a way to deliver your hurt. I had to share this bad news with my mom not because of a book, but because she deserves my truth. So parents, when you ask your kids the deep questions be prepared for deeper answers. The answer may not be pretty, but you can help your child get out of an ugly situation. My mom has been beyond supportive even in the midst of such an ugly decision. Once the truth is revealed, this is an opportunity for a parent and a child to recover together. Full recovery is necessary so a decision like that would never be made again. My last portion of advice to the parent and the child is to love each other through the process. Get it all out, tell the entire truth so this pain will never be revisited.

I write this story in *this* book because I know I'm not the only female that has ever felt that way. I know I'm not the only female that ever did something stupid, crazy, and embarrassing. I know what it feels like when you do something and believe you will never be able to recover from it. Young ladies, please listen, every decision you make takes you towards your destiny or pulls you away from it. Please be careful of doing things that you know you should not do. Maybe you believe you will never get caught, and maybe you're right. There's a name that God goes by, which is El'Roi which means the God who sees me. Your parents may never catch you. You may never get in trouble with any adults. But the truth is, God sees you. You can never hide from God. You can never climb a mountain too high that He won't see you. You can never go too low in the valley that He won't find you.

He sees it all. I hope my generation gets to a place in their lives that we become more concerned about what God sees, than whether or not we get caught by our parents. If I would have never told my mom, she would've never found out. The reason why I had to share my ugly truth with the woman I love is because God commands us to do that. So young ladies, have those tough conversations with your parents. I know you don't want to tell them. I know you don't want to be exposed or embarrassed, but the truth really sets you free. You will no longer have to put on a mask at a place called home because you shed your ugly truth. I know what it feels like to judge yourself over and over again. I know what it feels like to replay the same silly decision in your head continually. I want to remind every female that's reading this book, no matter what you have done: YOU ARE FORGIVEN. My biggest challenge wasn't whether or not God forgave me, but it was me really forgiving myself. Many times we ask God to forgive us and He does just that. He forgives us and completely lets it go. Meanwhile, we constantly beat ourselves up for doing wrong things, even when God has already forgiven us. For example, let's say a person committed a crime, and they go to jail for it. A good lawyer is hired to represent you and you are found guilty for the crime you have committed, but instead of getting the time you deserve, you get a shorter sentence. That's how I look at what God has the ability to do. *Even though we are guilty of doing wrong things, God doesn't give us what we deserve, He gives us another chance by forgiving us when we ask for forgiveness.* Asking for forgiveness is a very important step in recovery because how can God help you if you never ask for His assistance in the situation? God **wants** to help. God wants to clean you up. God wants to restore you. God wants to redeem you. When God forgive us but we don't forgive ourselves, it's like we are still in prison but the gate is WIDE open for us to walk out to be free. Don't ever waste an opportunity to be free when God has given you another chance.

You have to forgive you.

This has been the hardest thing for me. I had to accept that God forgave me for such a horrible decision. God is not like our friends or family, He forgives. The word FORGIVE means to wipe the slate clean, to pardon, to cancel a debt. That's amazing news! How would you feel if you owed someone $50,000 and they said don't worry about paying them back? Excited right? Exactly, the truth of the matter is that we ALL had a debt to pay. Sin was a debt to all mankind, and no one has enough funds to pay for themselves. So God sent a man named Jesus to come and settle the debt on our behalf. You no longer have to stay in sin or remain feeling guilty for what you did in your past because JESUS has settled the debt. When people try to bring up what you did in your past, just remind them that your debt is paid because of what Jesus did on the cross. If you truly ask God to forgive you, God said you are forgiven and that's all. Hebrews 8:12 says, "For I will forgive their wickedness and will remember their sins no more!" Think about that. God says that not only will He forgive you for your sins, but He will also forget them. God is so much better than people. People will always try to bring up what you did, how you did it, and why you did it. God isn't like that, once it's forgiven it's forgotten. Instantly I think about a man named

Peter in the Bible who denied he knew Jesus. Jesus still forgave him. God called him out, and he's calling you out too because you're forgiven. Have you ever been betrayed, deceived, or forsaken by someone you loved? That hurts, right? Well God's relationship with us isn't based on what we do to Him; it's based on His commitment to us. God knew what you were going to do before you knew it. He already knew what Peter was going to do before Peter knew. That's the same with us. Like I said in the previous chapter: God made us. It doesn't matter how big or small your sins are, God will forgive you. God's forgiveness doesn't have favorites. You can't hide from God. No matter how hard you try, it's won't work. God wants you to come to Him about your problems *first*, instead of others. You are forgiven. Not only do you have to believe that you are forgiven, you must also ACCEPT that you are forgiven.

Ladies, we must understand that salvation is a key point in forgiveness. Meaning if you haven't accepted Christ as your Lord and Savior then you need to do so. It's very simple. All you must do is say Romans 10:9 which says, "If you confess with your mouth and believe in your heart that Jesus raised him up from the dead then you shall be saved". On the other hand, we must understand that just because God forgives us for the things we do, it's not a pass to do whatever we want. I believe that when we say we want to live for God and have a *real* relationship with God our behaviors have a significant change. When we have real relationships with God, real transformation takes place in our everyday choices.

YOU ARE FORGIVEN.

Let's Pray:

Thank you, God, for forgiving me. Even when I don't deserve your grace or mercy you still give it to me. God help me to forgive myself and to walk boldly in your purpose for my life. I know I am forgiven because of your son, Jesus Christ paying the price on my behalf. God, I accept you as my Lord and Savior because I confess with my mouth that I am a sinner that needs to be saved. Save me through faith, God, and may I never return to a place of bondage. May I be free because who the son sets free is free indeed. God I believe that you raised Jesus up from the dead. Thank you for forgiving me and giving me the most precious gift ever: a relationship with you, God.

Amen.

"LADIES' LIFELINES"

SCRIPTURES TO REMEMBER

"For if you forgive other people when they sin against you, your heavenly Father will also forgive you. ₁₅But if you do not forgive others their sins, your Father will not forgive your sins."

Matthew 6:14-15

"Therefore I say to you, her sins, which are many, are forgiven, for she loved much. But to whom little is forgiven, the same loves little."

Luke 7:47-48

"If we confess our sins, He is faithful and just to forgive us our sins and to cleanse us from all unrighteousness."

1 John 1:9

JOURNAL

YOU ARE FORGIVEN.

What are the areas of your life that you need to ask for forgiveness in? Who do you need to ask to forgive you? What are some things you have done that you need to forgive yourself for?

_____

_____

_____

_____

_____

_____

_____

_____

_____

_____

_____

_____

_____

_____

_____

_____

_____

FACT NUMBER TWO

_____

_____

_____

_____

_____

_____

_____

_____

_____

_____

_____

_____

_____

_____

_____

_____

_____

_____

_____

_____

_____

FACT NUMBER TWO

FACT NUMBER TWO

you ARE...

LOVED.

The desire to be loved comes from not only those you want to have a relationship with, but it could be family members as well. What about those that really don't feel love from those that are related to them? I will never forget when I found out about what one of my peers who was going through something really tough. It was one of the most challenging things in his life. He found out as a teenager that the lady he's been living with all of his life isn't his real mother. The lady that's actually raising him isn't his biological mother, but it's his biological sister. What a shocker right? He was deeply hurt once he heard the real truth. He continued to ask his sister, "Why would our mom just leave us like this?" and "Why didn't you tell me?" So many questions began to come across his mind and his sister just listened to them all. That same teenage boy began to say, "My own mother doesn't love me." I had to remind him that even though his real mother isn't a part of his life, he is still loved. I had to show him the good in the midst of the bad. Even though his mom left him, his sister still stayed when she could've left. I want every young lady to understand that you shouldn't cry too long over the people that left, but *thank God for the people that stayed.* Be thankful for those that God has sent in your life to make up for the lack in your life. Someone in your life may have dropped you, but the good news is that God will always send someone else to help you recover from your fall. Your life will come with challenges, but God will send the right people to help you defeat every obstacle that comes your way.

Believe it or not, I believe everyone desires to be loved. Are you the female that doesn't feel loved? Do you feel like everyone constantly talks down on you? It's important to view love from God's way and not the way of the world. I know what it means to do anything to be *loved* by a person that doesn't even *like* you. Many ladies are trying to be accepted by people that have no interest in them at all. If that is the case, the question is **why do we run after people to feel complete?** There are many reasons why. One reason many ladies run after a male that has little or no interest in them is because the majority of their life was filled with rejection. Females that have been rejected are willing to compromise who they are to be loved for just a little while. Ladies that's a dangerous way to love and live. You try your best to be loved the world's way instead of God's way, but the world's definition of love will always leave you disappointed. The world views love as affection, so when we feel affection from others we believe we are loved. Most people tell other people that they love them just because it sounds good or fulfilling. The root word of "affection" is "affect" which means *to touch or to feel,* which means this love is based on the senses. We love only when it makes us feel good. **Ladies be careful of the desire to only want a feeling for a moment, instead of wanting the right love for eternity.** Just because you don't feel God's love physically that doesn't mean you're not loved. God's love is not a feeling, it's an action. God's love is perfect and it will never fail even when you feel like your entire life is a failure. I remember when my mentor, shared the story about a girl he grew up with, but she moved away to another state. When she relocated, she met this guy and fell in love with him. They did everything together and based on him explaining the story, I do mean *everything.* They saw each other every day, went on dates weekly, they stayed on the phone all night, and so much more. Well, one day the young man found a "better" girlfriend and he didn't want to be with her anymore. They had been together for 6 years and he wakes up one day and decides he wants the other girl instead of her. She's completely hurt and doesn't know what to do. She began to call and **beg** for him to take her back. The young man refuses to take her back because he has moved on. That night she's at home in her room and she calls him one more time and he answers. She says please take me back, and for the final time he says NO! He goes on to say that he regrets dating her because his new girlfriend is prettier, nicer, and she understands him more. He then says to his ex-girlfriend "F*** you" and tells her to NEVER call him back again in her life. Now at this moment the young lady is hurt beyond words. She feels like her world has been taken away from her. She's crying non-stop and her emotions are all over the place. She texted her ex-boyfriend and says "I will always love you, have a great life!" She takes out a gun from under her bed and she blows her brains out right in her room. Life is over for this young lady because she no longer felt love from the person she gave her entire world to. Be careful who you give your heart to. If you give your heart to the wrong person, you won't receive love in return, you'll receive death.

A good heart in the hands of the wrong person is *always dangerous.*

This young lady that killed herself had a bright future and so much going for herself. She allowed someone else to control her future because he decided to leave. Never put your future in the hands of someone else. Remember I said in the story that she began to beg for him to take her back. You never should have to beg someone to love you. Real love isn't begging anyone to love you. Ladies, never feel like you have to reward people to spend time with you, care for you, and give attention to you. Receiving God's gift of love is more than enough. You are loved by God; God sacrificed his son for us. Just because we don't see God in a physical form that doesn't mean he doesn't love us. We must stop wanting to see everything and feel everything. Yes, we are human and at times the devil will want us to think that we are not loved. When you think that, immediately come back to this chapter and remind yourself that God's love is not a feeling, it's an action. Ladies, you don't have to settle in your expectations to be liked or loved. You don't have to compromise in what you believe in to be accepted into someone else's world. God has a plan for your life and he has someone for you that will not only match your expectations, but will also supersede them...but you must trust God with the searching process. Many times we find ourselves growing impatient in the process.

Know that you are worth the wait.

Sometimes those that are single become easily bored without someone special in their life, but the season of singleness shouldn't be a time to search, but it should be *a time for you to fall in love with yourself.* If you don't love yourself, the love from others will never matter. How do you expect to fall in love with someone else if you haven't completely loved yourself first? It takes time to really get to know someone for who they truly are. God didn't say He loves us and left it there. He showed us His love by sending His

son Jesus Christ to come die, so we can live. If that's not love,
I don't know what is. You can never get so caught up on the
three words that people utter out of their mouths: "I Love You."
But those words must have a following in action. Real love isn't
having someone beat you verbally, emotionally, mentally, and
certainly not physically. I can recall a time when a lady came to
an event and shared her story. She calls herself a "survivor." She
had been engaged for over 20 years and was physically beaten
for 19 of the 20 years. Every time she was physically abused,
within the next few hours, her fiancé said, "I only hit you because
I love you and I want you to do better." For 19 years, this woman
viewed love with a slap or a punch. **But that wasn't real love.** I
want to challenge the female that is reading this book. You are
in a relationship and your life is dependent on it. Get out of this
relationship before you get out of this world too soon. Accept the
truth about your current relationship that is deadly and not Godly.
I know you may be afraid to walk away from something that
you had every intention to stay with for a lifetime. But God said
there is more and better for you. Stop calling your relationship

love when it's really a prison that keeps you on lock down for emotionally, mentally, and even possibly physically. When you decide to get out of the prison of that relationship, you will appreciate the freedom that you have never experienced. Leaving the jail cell in that relationship is only a sign that you love yourself too. Not another day should you give other people permission to put you on lock down in their prison that only benefits them.

Get free now and love the person in the mirror. Loving yourself properly is a requirement to loving other properly. You will never be able to love other fully until you first love yourself. Many marriages will never survive because they came into the marriage not fully loving themselves and attempted to love their spouse fully. It is hard to give 100 percent to *someone else* when you only have 50 percent in yourself. **You can't give what you don't have.** You may feel like God doesn't love you because you have done something that didn't please God. Know that He will still loves you. Remember the second chapter and that you are forgiven.

You must remember that. If you've ever doubted your own worth, or don't know where to go, or you're losing heart. God is saying to you, "You are important enough to Me to justify the death of My Son. I want to have a close and intimate relationship with you."Don't wait another minute. Run. Yes, run to His arms right now. Let Him whisper these words to you, "I love you, I love you." Ladies,

YOU ARE LOVED.

Let's Pray:

Thank you God, for sacrificing your one and only son to show us that you love us. God, I will be more open to see action instead of looking for a feeling when it comes to love. Help me understand the real definition of true love, which is your love. Your love is not the world's way it's the right way. I thank you for loving me and protecting me even when I didn't think I was loved. God help me love myself the away you love me. God, I don't feel very lovable. No matter how hard I try, I mess things up and end up feeling guilty and unlovable. But today I'm going to take a chance on You. I'm going to assume You really mean it when You say I am precious in Your sight, and You love me. I throw myself into Your arms. Thank You, thank You for a love that is bigger than all my mistakes. In Jesus' Name,

Amen.

"LADIES' LIFELINES"

SCRIPTURES TO REMEMBER

"God shows his love for us in that while we were still sinners, Christ died for us."

Romans 5:8

"I love those who love me, and those who seek me diligently find me."

Proverbs 8:17

"Know therefore that the LORD your God is God; he is the faithful God, keeping his covenant of love to a thousand generations of those who love him and keep his commandments."

Proverbs 8:17

"For God so loved the world, that he gave his only Son, that whoever believes in him should not perish but have eternal life."

John 3:16

JOURNAL

YOU ARE LOVED.

What is love to you? Who do you love? Have you ever felt unloved? If so, what happened?

_____

_____

_____

_____

_____

_____

_____

_____

_____

_____

_____

FACT NUMBER THREE

you ARE...

VALUABLE.

It's wonderful that God clearly proves our value throughout the Bible. Anything you can imagine and place value in on this Earth is unparalleled to how God feels about us. Think for a moment about diamonds. They are one of the most precious items in creation. They are rare, beautiful and highly prized, but they are *nothing* compared to how God values us. Does God really think you and I are more precious than diamonds? We — who trip and fall and fail more often than we care to admit? It's so easy to make an assertion without any facts to back it up. If you stopped right there and assumed this title is true — that you really are more precious than diamonds, you could go away feeling better about yourself without having any foundation on which to base your good feelings. And how long would that last? Not very long, I'm afraid. So, if we're going to compare ourselves to diamonds, how much is a diamond worth anyway? In 2013, a nearly 60-carat flawless pink diamond called the "Pink Star" was auctioned off for $83.2 million. That's a lot of money right? That made it the most expensive jewel or diamond ever sold at an auction. The most precious diamond, we're told, is part of the British Crown

Jewels collection. Experts say this gem cannot be valued — it's calculated to be approximately 3.5 times the wealth of the whole world! These diamonds are incredibly valuable to us, but to God, diamonds just aren't that precious. Nor are other costly stones, or even gold. After all, in Heaven, He uses gold for paving streets, pearls for gates instead of wrought iron (Revelation 21:21) and gems to decorate the foundations of the Heavenly City (Revelation 21:19). But you? Now, that's another matter. God has formed many diamonds, but **He made only one you**. You are unique. You are unlike anyone else who has ever lived or ever will live. He made you because He wants someone exactly like you. He has plans for you. You may be feeling pretty worthless right now, or beaten down. Life has probably thrown more at you than you feel you can handle. You don't feel worth as much as a rhinestone, let alone a diamond. Take heart! "You are precious in my eyes," God says, "and I love you" (Isaiah 43:4). God never said He loved a diamond, but He does say He loves you.

Don't feel it?

Just think about this: We are so precious to God that He sent His only Son, Jesus, to this Earth to die so you and I wouldn't have to suffer because of the way we have messed up in our lives of sin. Author David Eckman, in Becoming Who God Intended, pictures God explaining this to us: "My Son is dying for you because you are worth a Son to Me." Just think about it for a moment: God says, *"You are worth a Son to Me!"*

Value is defined as something that has worth. What do you consider valuable in your life? Who do you consider valuable in your life? When many hear of valuable items they instantly think of diamonds. Diamonds are indeed valuable, but I have found some interesting facts about diamonds. The value of a diamond is also measured by its condition. Many times, just like diamonds if we are not careful we can judge others based on their condition. Did you know that the value of a diamond is decreased if it's crushed? Diamonds that are whole are considered more valuable.

Do you think you're not valuable because you have been crushed so many times, by your husband, boyfriend, friends, or family members? Life will crush you and so will people. It's important that you deal with the crushing the right way. When you experience being crushed in life, it is not an opportunity for you to have a pity party. You must rise again. You must take the broken pieces from your past and your present situations and give it to God. Pieces in the hands of God are safe. God has the ability to take your brokenness and turn it into a blessing for someone else. God can create a masterpiece with your broken piece. Maybe you say "not my broken pieces..." Yes, yours. Never get to a place in your life that you have been crushed so deeply that you believe you can't bounce back. Romans 8:28 says, "For **we** know that all things work together for good to them that love God, to them who are the called according to his purpose." This scripture informs us that everything (good and bad), will work out for our good no matter what. The key word in this scripture is "we." Who is the "we?" We is referred in this scripture as believers. I want to encourage every female that's a believer in Christ that this scripture is talking about you. If you are not believer, this scripture is not making reference to you. It is for those who have a sincere relationship with Jesus Christ. There are benefits as a believer. One of those benefits according to scripture, is that all of your broken moments, painful experiences, and hurting times is setting you up for something greater. Remember this is for believers only. So don't you ever feel like you are wasting your time having a relationship with Christ because it pays off. I never said your walk with Christ would be easy, but it will be worth it because *you are worth it.* The key component as a benefit of being a believer is that the believer must love God. You can't have a great ending from your pain without first establishing an authentic loving relationship with Jesus Christ. A used car is a vehicle that has previously had one or more retail owners. Used cars are sold through a variety of outlets. Some of us are like used cars that feel as if our value has decreased because we have experienced tough times. Some feel like they are like a vehicle, up for sale, ready to be bought by a bidder at a cheaper price. Used cars don't cost as much to buy. Stop viewing yourself as a cheap vehicle. You have value.

Never put yourself on the clearance shelf.

Ladies, know you are not on sale for a discounted rate. If any male really loves you he will be willing to pay full price for you. Never allow anyone to convince you that you are worth less than what you really are.

Are you the female that feels like your own family doesn't think you are valuable?

We must understand that at times we will make bad decisions, but we are still valuable. There will be times that our bad thinking will land us in the wrong places. I want every young lady to understand that you don't have to stay in the dirt. Get up and clean up. Brush yourself off and understand that you still have value. In my previous book, I wrote about how I also thought I wasn't valuable. I didn't believe I was worth it, but all of that changed once I began to learn about **who** I was and **whose** I was. Once you accept the truth that God has written in His word about your worth, you will then accept the facts about your value. As discussed in a former chapter when I talked about the embarrassing act of me caving in to peer pressure by my ex-boyfriend, at that time in my life, I didn't know my worth. When you really don't know who you are, it's easy to do what others say even when you know better. I thought I could never recover from feeling worthless and feeling like nothing at times, but I DID! I had to really sit down and talk to God once I began to really have a made up mind that I wanted to do better. I began to accept His word that I am still valuable no matter what mistakes I've made. I had to accept in my mind and embrace in my heart that when others may call me nasty, when others may ask "what was she thinking?" God says it's okay, my daughter. Erion, I still love you, and you are forgiven. Just as I had to accept that God still sees my value (even after a really ugly situation) you must do the same. You must do same in your own life. Young lady, maybe you lost your virginity, maybe you wanted to commit suicide, maybe you also showed your body in an inappropriate way, or whatever it may be, GOD can still restore you after the mess you've been in.

Are you the female that doesn't have a father in your life to let you know you are valuable?

I grew up without my dad as well. I want to give you hope if you don't have a father figure in your life. My dad and I didn't have a relationship, but in the past year things have changed. I never thought we would have the relationship we have today. We talk on the phone, we text one another, and the best part of it all is we forgave one another. Even now my dad builds me up, he says positive things, and sends random messages of how much he loves me. I must honestly say I really appreciate those small things because it only reconfirms what God has already said about me.

Your value isn't based on what you experience. It is completely contingent upon who God is. You are the daughter of the Most High King. Know your worth. In modern day, the average princess doesn't live in an apartment, a home, or even a mansion. Their address is connected to a castle. Before that princess ever was birthed, her end was predictable, simply because of who her dad is. Her dad's position in power, paved the way for her to live in royalty forever. Just like that princess is set up to live a life in great value, so are you. God, the King of Kings, has paved the way for you to live in the kingdom in a royal way. Ladies of all ages, you will never settle for a peasant when you've been created to have a prince. Know that royalty is in your bloodline. You have been created from the cloth of the kingdom of God. God has high expectations for your life, so never lower them for anyone that doesn't fit into the plan He has for your life. So if you are struggling to find your value, recognize that...

YOU ARE VALUABLE.

Let's Pray:

God thank you for still seeing my worth even when I didn't value myself. Thank you Lord for being willing to forgive me when others wouldn't for the things I have done. God help me remember that I am valuable no matter what has happen to me in my past. God thank you for helping me understand who I am in you and not in others. God I accept your word for my life, that I am worthy because of what Jesus Christ has done.

Amen.

"LADIES' LIFELINES"
SCRIPTURES TO REMEMBER

"Look at the birds of the air; they do not sow or reap or store away in barns, and yet your heavenly Father feeds them. Are you not much more valuable than they?"

Matthew 6:26

"Are not five sparrows sold for two pennies? Yet not one of them is forgotten by God. Indeed, the very hairs of your head are all numbered. Don't be afraid; you are worth more than many sparrows."

Luke 12:6-7

"Greater love has no one than this that someone lay down his life for his friends."

John 15:13

"Do you not know that your bodies are temples of the Holy Spirit, who is in you, whom you have received from God? You are not your own; you were bought at a price. Therefore, honor God with your bodies."

1 Corinthians 6:19-20

JOURNAL

YOU ARE VALUABLE.

What has happened in your life that causes you to feel worthless at times? What's the most valuable thing you have? Who is the most valuable person you are connected to? And why?

_____

_____

_____

_____

_____

_____

_____

_____

_____

_____

_____

_____

_____

_____

_____

_____

_____

_____

_____

FACT NUMBER FOUR

FACT NUMBER FOUR

you ARE...

UNIQUE.

You really don't have to travel far to discover just how much God loves diversity and variety. Think about it: God made over 300,000 species of beetles. Now some might call that creative overkill. But God loves variety. Did you know that in one cubic foot of snow there are 18 million individual snowflakes and not one of them are alike? And while we can't tell the difference, it's just snow to us, God notices and created each one of them. God likes variety in people too. If you ever had to wait for an airplane or stand in line at WalMart, you'll see all sorts of unique and peculiar people. God made every one of them individually, and when we look in the mirror we see just how great and different we are. The Bible says, "You made all the delicate, inner parts of my body and knit me together in my mother's womb. Thank you for making me so wonderfully complex! Your workmanship is marvelous – and how well I know it." (Psalm 139:13-14 NLT) This verse has three foundational truths on how God created us.

First, you're unique. There's no one else like you in the entire world. There has never been and there never will be. You are the one and only, and God broke the mold after he made you. Now, some look at me and say, "Thank God." Personally, I'm not really sure how I should take that, but...

God doesn't create carbon copies

only originals.

If you were to travel the entire length and breath of our planet you wouldn't find anyone else with the same footprint, fingerprint, or voice print. You are unique.

Did you know your brain can compute about 15,000 decisions every second? Did you know your nose can smell 10,000 different odors? This is how uniquely you were made. You are special to God. You matter to Him. God made you unique.

Second, you're wonderfully complex. You're so complex you're even a mystery to yourself. Sometimes we say or do things that completely surprise us and we wonder, "Where did that come from?" God calls you complex and the enemy calls you complicated. Never get the two confused. Complex is defined as "consistent of many different and connected parts." Complicated is defined as "consistent of interconnecting parts that are completely tangled." Satan's job is to convince you that you are not unique, but you are complicated. Many of us do not really embrace us being different because we are afraid of being the only one that does, says, or acts a certain way. I can recall when one of the volunteers in 29:11 Mentorship Program struggled with this in a major way. She informed us that as a 20-year-old young lady, she felt complicated. She didn't go to the clubs, she didn't drink, didn't smoke, she simply wanted to be around other people her age that love God. This way of living isn't normal in her generation. Some of her peers would ask her to go to certain places. She would agree to it, but would be completely uncomfortable. She was attempting to fit in when she was born to stand out. The enemy began to play with her mind and she began to believe that something was wrong with her. Why she doesn't like drinking…Why she doesn't like smoking…Why she doesn't like the latest song? She had to accept the fact that she wasn't complicated…but she was complex. She was complex because she was different from what others normally see. She is 20, no kids, a virgin, loves God, only listens to gospel music and her own generation says "that's not normal." She has finally accepted the fact that being chosen to be different comes with a price to pay. That price is being able to be by yourself and still not feel alone. That price is when everyone else is doing wrong, you stand up for right. That price is being called "the church girl" instead of "the cool girl." Being different will cost you a lot. Being complex and being complicated have something in common. They both are connected to parts, the difference is how that connection looks. **When you are complex, you are connected with structure. When you are complicated you are connected in chaos.**

Third, you were created for a purpose. God created everything in the world for a purpose, including you. You're not here by accident. You didn't just evolve. You're not merely the result of a biological process. You're who you are because God made you, and God has a plan and purpose for your life. God made you for a reason. It was His idea, and God doesn't make mistakes. **You were planned before you were born.** God didn't just sit down and randomly access a bunch of components and threw them together and out you came. God purposefully and personally designed you. You are unique and God wanted you to **be uniquely you**, and that is the you God wants to offer to the world.

Every human being that has ever lived, or ever will live, is unique. Uniqueness is defined by being the only one of its kind; unlike anything else. You are truly one of a kind. Ladies, you are an exclusive copy that could never be duplicated. We all know that, we, as humans, share the usual bits and pieces that most of us have in common, such as certain essential body parts — a head, a heart, a brain, and so on. But the similarity ends there. Your life experiences thus far have made you the person you are today. The way you were brought up by your parents and the things that you learned in your childhood have come together to make you different from everyone else. You may have learned some things in a similar way to other children, such as having respect for authority, the need to clean up your room, or to brush your teeth twice a day, and so on. Yet you will have also learned many things that other children did not, such as how to care for a rabbit, or play a musical instrument, or build a fort in the woods, or solve complicated math equations.

It is the combination of everything that you have learned and the various things that you have done that make you truly different from everyone else on this planet. Others may share some of your talents and abilities, but there is no one who is identical to you. It is rather like an artist painting a picture; even if another artist were to copy the picture as closely as possible it would never be identical. Different brush strokes or combinations of paint would have been used, and each masterpiece is its own.

Are you the female that wants to fit in? Are you more concerned about being liked than being unique? I want you to think about this: Remember about one hundred years ago women couldn't vote, couldn't hold CEO positions, and couldn't even have their own bank account. According to research many women couldn't go to college (less than 6% of women over the age of 25 had completed 4 years of college even in 1940). However, women made changes. In 1986, females outnumbered the males earning master's degrees in the United States. In order for such a great shift in history, someone had to embrace the fact that women were, and continue to be, different.

We must keep in mind that God made us all different. Some of us will be teachers, writers, business owners, a house wife, or something else. The truth is we are all different and we will do different things no matter what others tell us. God made us all with a different DNA.

God wants us to be who He created us to be. When we are unique we are unlike anything else, no matter what you hear from others, God says you are different. He doesn't want two of the same type of thinkers. **Think different and dream bigger!** It doesn't matter what people say when you're being yourself. It ONLY matters what God has to say. I remember when I first started following God. My former friends at the time invited me to their party and I went. Parties for teens mostly consist of twerking, cussing, and much more if there's not the proper supervision. I remember sitting down because of my new found respect for God and even for myself. I was the only teenager sitting down while everyone else was dancing. One of my peers asked me, "why are you not dancing?" I simply told them "it's a new me." Following that, I also attended another party for a teen and did the same exact thing. One may read this and began to think, Erion must think she's better than others? No, I don't believe I'm better than anyone, but I do believe now as a young lady, there's a way to carry myself. Maybe you ask the question, "well why attend the party in the first place?" That's a good question. I attended those parties because I do understand I am child of God now and I share the responsibility as a believer to make sure I still am reachable for those that want help and those that want better. Please understand I did not go to the party and attempt to bring others to Christ. I was simply going to be a light in a dark place. I don't believe we have to preach Jesus down their throat for them to get the message. I believe that if we simply live our life the right way, those that need Christ will ask for our assistance.

As Christians we should never be so distant from people that

don't have a relationship with God because we don't want to

be around their dysfunction. We all have been dysfunctional at

a time in our lives. No one was born with a relationship with

God, and all of us that do have a relationship with God had to

develop one. When I refused to dance like a girl gone wild or do

what everyone else was doing, I wasn't being arrogant, I simply

understand that I am different now. I had to be okay with being

unique, regardless of whether my peers agreed or disagreed with

my decision not to dance. Once you begin to live for God your

circle will change. Since that last party, none of my peers every

invited me to a party like that ever again. And guess what? **No**

invitation is ok. When you're understand you are different and

unique you are not offended by the opinion of others. Accept that

YOU ARE UNIQUE.

Let's Pray:

Father thank you for creating me differently. God forgive me for worrying about what others say when I only should've been more concerned about what you think. God help me be bold in being different for you. God never let me be so distant from those that don't know you that I don't have an opportunity to help when needed. God let me be able to love myself in a way that totally accepts me being completely unique.

Amen.

"LADIES' LIFELINES"
SCRIPTURES TO REMEMBER

"Before I formed you in the womb I knew you, and before you were born I consecrated you; I appointed you a prophet to the nations."

Jeremiah 1:5

"But when he who had set me apart before I was born, and who called me by his grace."

Galatians 1:15

"My son, do not walk in the way with them; hold back your foot from their paths."

Proverbs 1:15

"So God created man in his own image, in the image of God created he him; male and female created he them."

Genesis 1:27

JOURNAL

YOU ARE UNIQUE.

What makes you different from others? Honestly, do you like being different? Yes or no? Explain. If you could change one thing about yourself, what would it be?

_____

_____

_____

_____

_____

_____

_____

_____

_____

_____

_____

_____

_____

_____

_____

_____

_____

_____

_____

_____

_____

FACT NUMBER FIVE

FACT NUMBER FIVE

FACT NUMBER FIVE

you
ARE...

BOLD AND **BEAUTIFUL.**

Ladies, do you ever wake up, take a good look in the mirror, and tell yourself, "No doubt about it—I'm fearfully and wonderfully made!" Maybe when you think about the kind of person you are, words like "average" or "not bad" come to mind. Sometimes you might see yourself as above average, but there are days when a closer look reveals insecurities and flaws that you can't ignore. If you ever consider yourself unremarkable or even ordinary, you're not seeing yourself as a result of God's divine creation. When we discover the truth that we are God's beautiful design,
it is overwhelming.

Genesis 1:27 reads, "God created man in his own image...male and female he created them." We often mistakenly equate this with just physical appearance. Only Jesus Christ is the expressed image of God's person, having the same nature (Colossians 1:15-17; Hebrews 1:3). God honored us by fearfully and wonderfully making the Word flesh (John 1:1, 14), clothing the Son of God with a body like ours; then clothing our fleshly body with a glory like His. But it is the soul of human beings that especially bears

God's image: mind, will, and emotion. God's image on us consists of knowledge, righteousness, and true holiness (Ephesians 4:24; Colossians 3:10).

You are bold and beautiful, when you **believe** everything that you have read before this chapter. Being bold is doing something unpredictable. Writing my first book and now completing my second book was unpredictable for some people and even for me at a time. When you understand that you're not bold by yourself, but **with God anything is possible!**

Scripture declares that we are beautiful and wonderful and nothing we do can add to or take away from that truth. We must decide to focus on Christ and trust Him. Scripture is teaching us that Christ loves us and has made us exactly how He wanted us to be for His plan for our lives. If we, as women, want to have the confidence that we are always seeking and overcome self-esteem issues, then we need to turn our focus onto the man who thought we were worthy enough to die for before we were ever born.

We must look to Christ and not to ourselves and fully embrace

what He has told us is true about who we are.

We are daughters of a king who loves us and *delights in who we are.*

So where do we go from there? Our problem is not our beauty, it

is that we are not fully satisfied in what His word says about how

we were made. I read a book about two years ago that had a

statement that changed my life. It says, "The secret to overcoming

insecurity is not by learning self-esteem but learning to deny self."

Scripture teaches us that we are to "deny ourselves and follow

Him" or as John 3:30 teaches, "He must increase and we must

decrease".

We have been taught to feel good about ourselves by putting

all of our time and energy into what we believe will make us

feel better, look better, or be more liked. But the Bible tells us the

opposite that we are to take our focus off of ourselves and onto

Christ. Focus on the Lord and allow Him to grow your confidence as you focus on His plan for your life.

Ladies for us to be bold in who we are, we must have confidence in God and not ourselves. Ladies don't ever forget you are beautiful which means you are of very high standard. We must have very high standards we have to be okay with saying "NO" to people that's not treating us as bold and beautiful. It's not about what they say about you, it's about what you answer to. For every lady that has read this book remembers who you are, there will be times that your flesh will want to forget. When your flesh wants to win, I would like for you to pick this book up and to keep in mind what God laid on my heart to tell you. Everything that you have done and experienced has made you bold and beautiful, even the good and the bad. It all has worked out for you becoming a BETTER YOU for the King of Kings.

LADIES, DON'T EVER FORGET...

you are...

☑ **NOT A MISTAKE.**
☑ **FORGIVEN.**
☑ **LOVED.**
☑ **VALUABLE.**
☑ **UNIQUE.**

Bold
AND BEAUTIFUL.

Let's Pray:

Dear Lord. Banish negative thinking from my life. Let me see myself through Your eyes: holy, forgiven, wonderfully made in your image. Surround me with your love so that I am truly beautiful to myself. God let me take to heart what I have read so that my whole life, as a lady, is changed forever.

Amen.

"LADIES' LIFELINES"

SCRIPTURES TO REMEMBER

"Charm can mislead, and beauty soon fades. The woman to be admired and praised is the woman who lives in the Fear-of-God. Give her everything she deserves! Festoon her life with praises!"

Proverbs 31:30

"Finally, be strong in the Lord and in the strength of His might."

Ephesians 6:10-11

"For I am bold enough to tell you only about what the Messiah has accomplished through me in bringing gentiles to obedience. By my words and actions."

Romans 15:18

JOURNAL

YOU ARE BOLD AND BEAUTIFUL.

Based on everything you have read in this book, which chapter stands out the most and why? Where do you go from here, as a female, in your life?

_____

_____

_____

_____

_____

_____

_____

_____

_____

_____

_____

_____

_____

_____

_____

_____

_____

_____

_____

_____

_____

_____

_____

_____

_____

_____

_____

_____

_____

_____

_____

_____

_____

_____

_____

_____

_____

_____

_____

_____

_____

_____

_____

FACT NUMBER SIX

stay connected

Thank you for purchasing Bold & Beautiful: Six Things Every

Female Needs To Know. Erion wants to stay connected to you!

Here are a few ways you can connect with Erion.

follow me on social media

 @ERION DAVISON

 @ERION_PD

 @ERION_PD

 @ERION14

WWW.ERIOND.ORG

ERIONKEEPRUNNING@GMAIL.COM

Ever wanted to write your own book? Ever want to get a book
published? If so, call 225.287.1344!